# ...And They Laughed Ha Ha, Ha Ha, Ha Ha

## Sylvia White

Parson's Porch Books
www.parsonsporchbooks.com

...And They Laughed Ha Ha, Ha Ha, Ha Ha

ISBN: Softcover 978-1-946478-59-7

Copyright © 2020 by Sylvia White

Assistance provided by Judy W. Proctor

All rights reserved. No part of this book may be reproduced or transmitted in any form or by any means, electronic or mechanical, including photocopying, recording, or by any information storage and retrieval system, without permission in writing from the publisher.

Story One
# Kooky Lucy

There was a lady named Lucy who lived in a place called Pleasant Village. She was always looking for a place to have fun. She began laughing at anything and laughing at anyone. But when she started laughing at the misfortunes of other people, she began to make people very upset and angry.

Because they thought she was unable to stop laughing they said that she was crazy. They began calling her Kooky Lucy. Can you believe the way Kooky Lucy laughed at the school boy who had skinned his knee?... And she laughed, "Ha ha," laughed "ha ha," and laughed "ha ha."

    Ha ha
    Ha ha
    Ha ha

She laughed at the spaghetti dinner Aunt Marie had prepared. She dropped both the spaghetti and serving bowl on the floor…And Kooky Lucy laughed, "Ha ha," laughed "ha ha," and laughed "ha ha".

    Ha ha
    Ha ha
    Ha ha

She laughed at the neighbor who fell from a ladder…
… And she laughed, "Ha ha", laughed "ha ha," and laughed "ha ha."

    Ha ha
    Ha ha
    Ha ha

Lucy said, "I'm going to help you put this ladder back up. But you have caused me to laugh so much that my sides hurt; and they simply won't stop hurting right now." And a little later, Lucy waved goodbye. And she laughed "Ha ha", laughed "ha ha," and laughed, "ha ha."

    Ha ha

    Ha ha

    Ha ha

When the landlord saw the broken window, he kicked her out of his house.
…And all of the people in Pleasant Village shouted "Hooray," shouted "hooray," and shouted, "hooray".

    Hooray
    Hooray
    Hooray

# Story Two
# Sobbing Susan

For people who liked to take walks, Pleasant Park would be the perfect place to walk. Tammy, Alice, and Jane chose to drive from their houses across the village just to spend time at Pleasant Park.

One day they decided to walk outside the park a short distance to the Yum Yum Ice Cream store. They had not walked very far when they heard some crying. As they walked closer toward the Yum Yum Ice Cream Store, they saw a lady digging in the dirt. They thought she was hurt. Tammy spoke up, "What's the matter?"

Susan, the dear lady who was crying, looked up at the three ladies and said, "Don't worry ladies, I'm not hurt. I cry all the time and don't know why. Now you can understand why people call me 'Sobbing Susan'".

Tammy, Alice, and Jane appeared at Susan's house the next day. They brought flowers to cheer up Susan.

Now this was very thoughtful; but Susan cried, "Boo hoo," cried, "boo hoo" and cried "boo hoo".

        Boo hoo
        Boo hoo
        Boo hoo

The next day Sobbing Susan's three new friends brought her flowers and tissues. They couldn't believe it when she asked for more tissues.

Susan thanked them, and then she cried, "Boo hoo," cried, "boo hoo," and cried "boo hoo".

      Boo hoo
      Boo hoo
      Boo hoo

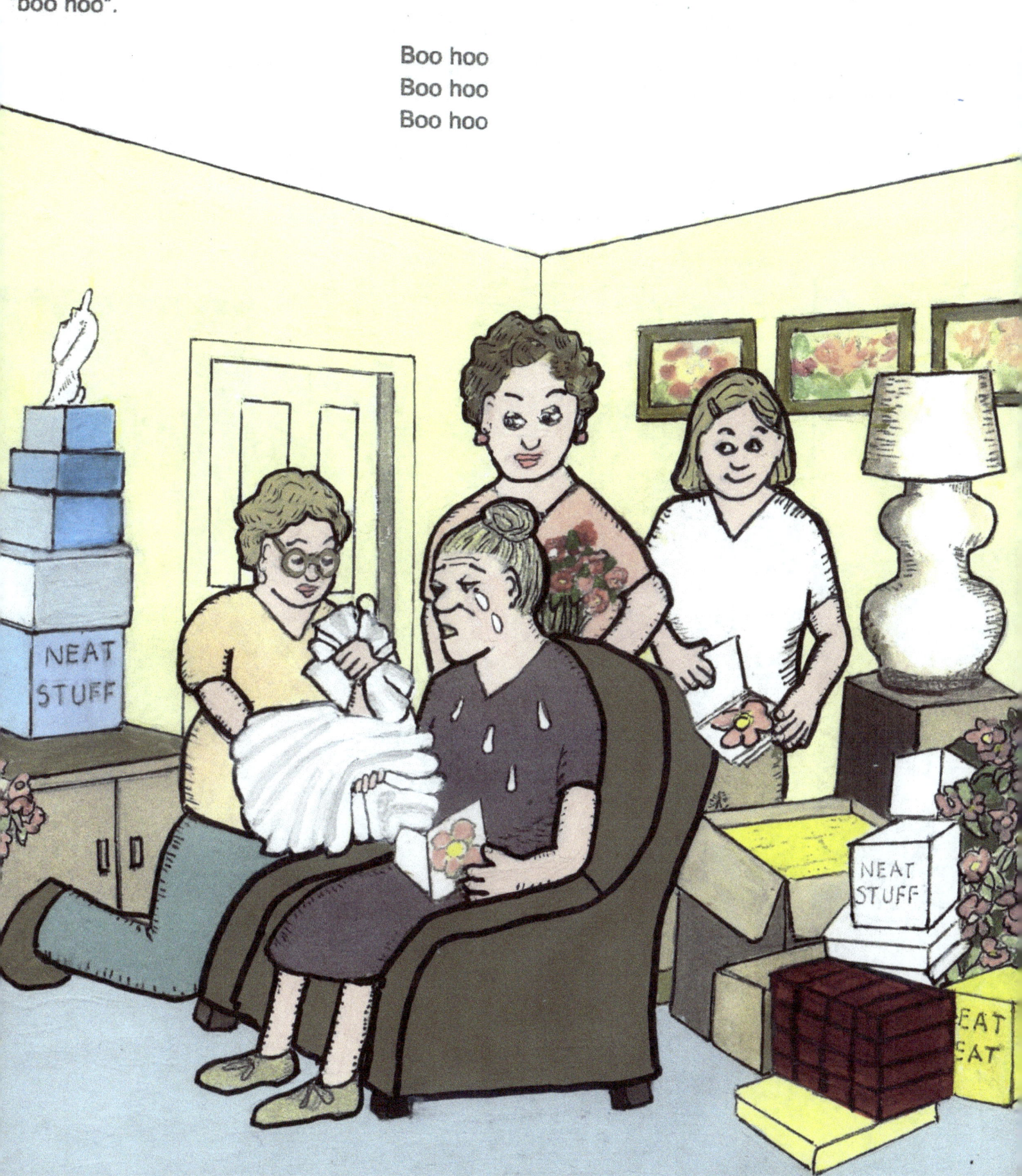

The next day Sobbing Susan's friends had a new TV delivered. Susan thanked them and then cried, "Boo hoo," cried, "boo hoo," and cried "boo hoo".

        Boo hoo
        Boo hoo
        Boo hoo

Then, while Susan was busy blowing her nose and wiping her tears, Tammy said, "Let's not look for more things to buy Susan."

I know what we can do," said Alice. "We can get a
        cat or a dog or both".

Susan and her three friends liked the idea of getting a pet. So off they drove to Pleasant Village Animal Shelter.

Susan picked out a cute, brown male dog and named him Champ. Then she chose a yellow female cat and named her Flopsy.

On their way back home, they bought Crunch Crunch dog food and Meow Meow cat food.

When they got back home, both Champ and Flopsy had a wonderful time happily frolicking around Susan's backyard.

　　… And Sobbing Susan stopped crying!

Staying at the Animal Shelter left little room for Champ and Flopsy to move about in large spaces. Here in Susan's backyard, they had fun running around bushes and chasing after rabbits.

Yes, it was a happy time in Susan's backyard. Susan's neighbors came over to visit. They were delighted to find that Susan had given up her crying ways.

Most days Champ and Flopsy were able to get along well with each other. But one day Champ tried to chase Flopsy. Now that was not a smart thing for Champ to do. All Flopsy had to do to get away from Champ was to find a tree. A small tree would be okay. Well, wouldn't you know it? Flopsy picked the tallest tree in the yard. When Flopsy climbed up the tree she chose to climb up to the very top limbs. All she had to do would be to perch herself on the very first limb of the tree. She just needed to be patient and wait for Champ to go away. Then she started to "me-ow, me-ow and me-ow". She was simply too scared to come down. Susan, Tammy, Alice and Jane called to Flopsy over and over, and over again. Alice brought a tall ladder from under Susan's back porch, but it was not long enough. Then Tammy pulled out her cell phone and called the fire department.

A group of Susan's neighbors gathered around the big tree to watch Flopsy's rescue. While they were watching, Patsy and Andrew Jones spoke to Susan about putting up a fence for Champ all in one day. Andrew said to Susan, "I have the day off tomorrow. I can build a fence for Champ. Would you like me to help you?" Patsy said, "Andrew is a great handy man, Susan." "Gee Andrew, I surely appreciate your offer," Susan said.

Then Andrew said, "After the fireman leave, show me where to put a fence. Then Patsy and I will come over tomorrow morning and build a fence for our friend Champ."

The next day Andrew and Patsy Jones drove over to Susan's house in Andrew's truck. They had been to Joe's Hardware Store and brought back fifty posts and wire fencing. Susan's job was to hold the fencing posts while Andrew attached the wires to the posts. Pasty decided that she was not needed yet and went inside Susan's house to visit Tammy, Alice, and Jane.

While the women were inside the house visiting, Andrew saw that he needed ten more posts. He asked Susan if she wanted to go with him to the hardware store, but Susan said, "No, I think I will go inside and have a visit with my three friends and Patsy."

When Andrew drove his truck to the hardware store, Susan walked up the stairs to the back porch. She heard the women inside talking and it was all about her. Susan stopped short of the back door and listened.

The first person Susan heard talking was Alice. Alice said, "Look she can't make any more excuses. Her foot has healed. I saw her walking back from the Yum Yum Ice Cream Store, and she was not using a cane."

Then Tammy spoke up, "With the messes she makes in her house after we have left her here alone, you would think she had not cleaned the house in years."

Jane said, "You try to teach her simple things. I don't think she will ever know how to toast bread without burning most of it; only the birds are happy to eat it then. And I gave up on trying to teach her how to flip a fried egg without dropping it on the floor."

Patsy spoke up, "You three dear ladies need to leave things undone here. Just stop coming over here anymore."

Tammy said, "That's hard for us to do, but we can't spend all our days here. We'll just need to leave her alone. It must be done."

Susan looked around and saw the green vines at the corner of the porch. Susan remembers that when she was younger, that it was a good place to hide when playing "Hide and Go Seek." Susan quickly scooted behind the vine leaves.

Susan said a silent, "Hooray" that she was not caught hiding from anyone yet. Susan turned her attention to Andrew and saw him unloading the ten posts. Then he began pumping air into the tires of his truck. When he had his back facing Susan, Susan crept out of her hiding place and joined Andrew. Andrew had no clue that she missed having a pleasant visit with the ladies inside her house.

Tammy, Alice, and Jane began gathering things that belonged in their own houses. There were things like sweaters, mops, mugs and extra dishes. They packed everything in Jane's car and waved goodbye.

Patsy was leaving too. She planned to go over to her house and bring back lots of snack crackers, peanut butter sandwiches, and ice tea.

All three helpers worked hard until it was time to take a break for the lunch Patsy brought.

After Andrew ate his lunch, he took the time to figure out how much longer it would be to finish their work. A little later Andrew returned to where Patsy and Susan were sitting. He put his face up close to Patsy and Susan and said, "Ladies, we ain't going to finish this here fence in one day. It's not possible. We have done ten pieces of fence now. Look ladies, we have fifty more pieces to do!"

"I am a man who always keeps his word, but the day is about halfway over. How is it possible for us to finish this fence in one day?"

Patsy said, "We have been moping around without much energy. Can't we push ourselves a little harder?"

Susan spoke up, "All we have to do is to call Yum Yum Pizza. That pizza store claims that their pizza can really give you lots of energy. I saw Bobby Harper sprain his ankle. When he ate some Yum Yum Pizza, he had enough energy to make a home run a short time later. Well," said Susan, "we need to order Yum Yum Pizza and have it delivered to my back yard. I'll call them right away."

Ten minutes after Susan, Patsy, and Andrew ate Yum Yum Pizza, they all had a burst of energy. It was unreal how fast they were able to put up the fence.

Hooray! The fence with sixty poles did get built in one day. It surely was a proud day for all three carpenters.

After Susan finished thanking Patsy and Andrew, she put Champ inside the fence and gave Champ some Crunch Crunch. After Champ wagged his tail, Susan knew he was happy.

After a long day, Susan was so tired she could hardly hold her head up to eat her supper of left-over sandwiches. Then Susan rested on her sofa and fell soundly asleep. Flopsy purred "Flopsy Music" and was sound asleep too.

Champ had a good reason for staying awake. He found out where Daisy Hop-along and Felix Hop-along lived. Champ began chasing Felix all around the lot. When Felix decided to stop running, he just squeezed under a hole at the bottom of the fence to be at home where he and Daisy Hop-along lived.

The next morning Susan woke up to the sound of Champ barking loudly. She let Champ inside and fed him Crunch Crunch. Next she fed Flopsy Meow Meow.

Susan's big chore for her day was baking a blackberry cobbler. Alice had brought the berries yesterday and had planned to help Susan bake a blackberry cobbler.

Could Susan trust Champ to stay in his new fenced-in space? He had been barking at the neighborhood dogs. There were two dogs outside looking over the fenced-in space. Susan did not want to cause any problems while she had dough on her hands. Champ should just stay inside for a while. Flopsy could be trusted to go most anywhere.

Susan started out washing the berries and then added some sugar. She put the bowl of blackberries aside. After this, Susan began working on the pastry part of the cobbler. Susan picked up the cookbook Alice had given her. She opened the book and read the pastry directions very carefully.

"Wow", Susan said. Susan read the directions again. "I have done exactly what the directions said to do. Look how sticky this dough is. I'm going to make the directions up for myself. I have never been able to read directions. I'm going to put more flour in this crust."

After Susan mixed the dough up, this time it was not so hard and not so gummy but just right. There was enough dough for the middle, for the four sides, and enough for the crisscrosses on the top. Susan poured the blackberries into the pan. Susan's final step was to set the oven at 425°.

Now Susan was ready to go outside to play with Champ. Some of the neighborhood k[ids] came over and played "Catch the Ball" with Champ.

On returning to the house, Susan smelled something burnt. Susan had a sinking "botto[m-] of-the stomach" kind of feeling; then she entered the house. Susan had forgotten to set t[he] timer to "off". Susan learned another lesson the hard way. The cobbler had burned in t[he] pan so badly that she did not think it could ever be cleaned. So Susan threw the pan awa[y.] Now I won't be able to share my cobbler with anyone. Susan's eyes were just dripping w[ith] tears.

Susan could not help it; tears dripped down her face. Then Susan cried, "Boo hoo," cri[ed] "boo hoo," and cried "boo hoo."

                    Boo hoo
                    Boo hoo
                    Boo hoo

One day Tammy called Patsy Jones and asked her how Susan was doing living alone and without any help. Patsy said, "I'm glad you called. I have big doubts about Susan. Sometimes she seems to be just fine, but the other day when I was driving by her house, I saw Susan sitting on the curb of Pleasant Street just crying her eyeballs out."

I stopped and asked if I could help her. "I have everything under control now," said Susan. "Those boys down the street should know better than to pick on younger kids. I told those boys I would have to call their parents if they acted that way again."

Then Susan cried, "Boo hoo", cried "boo hoo", and cried "boo hoo".

       Boo hoo
       Boo hoo
       Boo hoo

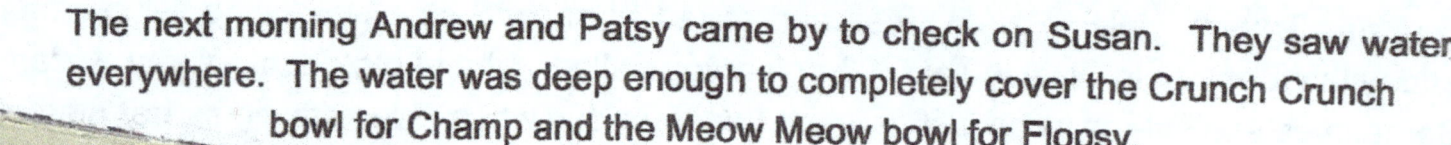

The next morning Andrew and Patsy came by to check on Susan. They saw water everywhere. The water was deep enough to completely cover the Crunch Crunch bowl for Champ and the Meow Meow bowl for Flopsy.

Then they saw Tammy and Alice trying to bail out Susan's tear water while Jane was trying to comfort Susan. "Wow! What is happening here?" asked Andrew.

Jane explained, "Susan has not stopped crying long enough to tell us why she is so sad. She has been crying since we have been here."

Alice spoke up, "Since we're standing in a pool of water, let's go up to the attic to talk some things over."

Tammy picked up her cell phone and asked, "Don't you think we need to call Dr. Brown?" Everyone nodded their heads to say, "Yes".

After Tammy described what was happening with Susan, Dr. Brown said, "I think I know how to help Susan. Bring her right over to my office."

When Susan entered Dr. Brown's office she had her cane and she was batting back tears.

"Now Susan, don't you cry on me," Dr. Brown said sternly. "You need to get your friends to help you go over to Pleasant Park and set up a campsite. Susan, you need plenty of fresh air and sunshine. Believe me, this will do wonders for you."

# Story Three
# Lucy and Susan

Tammy, Alice, and Jane came to Susan's the next day. They helped Susan Pack a wagon with a tent, hammock, clothes, and food for Champ and Flopsy.

As Susan began to think about this move to the park, she had missed feeling. She did not know any of the people who would be camping there. Susan was frightened by strangers.

When Susan began to cry, Tammy spoke up, "We've had enough fixing up around here. Let's walk over to the Yum Yum Ice Cream Store. A double dipped ice cream cone would be a winner for us. It's time for a break."

After Tammy, Alice, and Jane returned to their homes and families, Susan spent most of her time unpacking more things. Then she decided to walk around looking over Pleasant Park, her new home. She took Champ with her while Flopsy remained sleeping in the hammock.

Susan took a walk around Pleasant Campground. After visiting with another camper, she returned to her campsite and sat down on a nearby bench.

Soon Kooky Lucy came by and said, "I can sit on this bench too. Just because it is close to your campsite does not make it your bench." When Susan heard this, she began to cry, "Boo hoo," cry, "boo hoo," and cry "boo hoo."

      Boo hoo
      Boo hoo
      Boo hoo

Kooky Lucy just respectfully left the scene.

The next morning she thought she should do what Dr. Brown said to do: Take in the sunshine and get plenty of fresh air.

After Susan's walk around the park, she sat down on her bench. Susan had not sat there very long when Kooky Lucy decided to sit there too. Sobbing Susan could not let this happen. Susan hopped up on the bench and held up her cane to whack Kooky Lucy on the head. Fortunately, Mr. Holly, the camp director, saw what was happening. He took out a whistle and began to blow it loudly.

The next day Susan took a walk around the campground; she stopped to visit some ducks near a small pond. Soon Kooky Lucy appeared. She was carrying a bucket with blackberries. Lucy said, "There are bunches of blackberries across from this pond. Let me give you some of my blackberries."

Susan lowered her head, shook it slowly back and forth and said in a tearful voice, "You had better leave me alone. I'm about to drown you with my tears." Kooky Lucy said, "I believe that if I stayed long enough, you would drown me with your tears."

After Lucy left, Susan continued crying. She cried "Boo hoo," cried "boo hoo," and cried "boo hoo".
        Boo hoo
        Boo hoo
        Boo hoo

Then Susan noticed that the little pond grew larger, larger, larger and the little stream grew wider, wider, wider.

The next morning Susan was at the duck pond when Tammy, Alice, and Jane came by for visit. After a friendly greeting, Susan said, "I met this lady named Kooky Lucy who laughs everyone. She keeps getting into my space and I don't know how to deal with her." Tamm said, "We know about Kooky Lucy; she's the talk of the town." Alice said, "We need to sho you how to shush her away." Jane said, "Susan, just hold your hands out wide and wa them wildly. Then shout this chant: "Shush, shush, shush, away. Shush the words you sa today!"

Susan practiced shushing over and over with her three friends. She told them how thank she was with their shushing lesson. She was sure that shushing would work. After h friends left, Susan had a chance to put shushing into action. Kooky Lucy came down pathway to the pond laughing and bouncing all around Susan. Then Susan stood up straig and broke into her shushing chant.

    "Shush, shush, shush, away.
    Shush the words you say today!"

Susan kept shushing until Lucy finally left. A few minutes later, Susan broke down in tears. She cried, "Boo hoo," cried "boo hoo," and cried "boo hoo."

    Boo hoo
    Boo hoo
    Boo hoo

The next day Susan was sitting at her usual place at the duck pond. Along came Kooky Lucy, shouting out like a commander, "Now Susan, I've got something important to say. Mr. Holly and friends of the playground committee are planning to put up a fruit and vegetable stand. People are asked to donate fruit and vegetables from their gardens. That should bring some good money to pay for a new swing set. For my part, I'm planning to pick blackberries".

"Wait, wait, wait" shouted Susan angrily. "You have not given me a chance to shush you, and I'm about to shush you now, do you understand?" Lucy moved toward Susan and stared into Susan's eyes. Then she said, "I understand completely."

So, Susan used her shushing chant again: "Shush, shush, shush, away. Shush the words you say today!" In response, Lucy quietly walked away.

After Lucy left, Susan cried, "Boo hoo," cried "boo hoo," and cried "boo hoo".
 Boo hoo
 Boo hoo
 Boo hoo

Then the pond grew larger, larger, larger. And the stream grew wider, wider, wider.

The next day Mr. Holly came by the pond and the stream. He saw Susan crying and walked over to where she was sitting. "Oh Susan," he said, "Is Lucy still causing you problems? I thought she was through laughing at you."

Susan wiped her eyes dry and tried to speak. Susan said, "Yes, Kooky Lucy has stopped laughing, but today she was laughing again and is now calling me stupid. You wouldn't know how hard it was to step away and not clobber her."

"Finally", Susan said, "I turned my back away from her and stomped out of the place. When I saw she had left, I returned to my crying here at the pond." Mr. Holly said, "We will spend some time talking about the problem, but for now, I have got to make some safety signs to put around all this water."

After Mr. Holly left, Susan began crying again and the pond grew larger, larger, larger. And the stream grew wider, wider, wider.

A little later, Lucy showed up with her bucket and headed toward the blackberry patch. On seeing Lucy, Susan stood up and shouted, "Stop, Lucy, stop! You can't go to the blackberry patch that way. Can't you tell; the stream is too wide and deep?"

Lucy thought for a moment and said, "I know where the shallow spots are. I'll take my chances." Then she laughed, "Ha ha", laughed, "ha ha" and laughed, "ha ha".

    Ha ha
    Ha ha
    Ha ha

At first Lucy did very well wading in the water. And she laughed, "Ha ha," laughed, "ha ha," and laughed "ha ha."

    Ha ha
    Ha..lp
    He..lp
    Blub blub
    Blub blub

"Never fear, never fear and never fear," shouted Susan. "I can swim. I can swim. I can swim."

Then Susan grabbed a small log and swam out to Lucy. Lucy grasped hold to the log and to Susan. Then they both made it back safely to shore.

Just as soon as Lucy and Susan stepped on the bank of the river, they gave each other a big hug. Campers from Pleasant Park came over to find out about the rescue. Even the ducks came over to see what was going on. They gave their usual quacks:

    Quack quack quack
    Quack quack quack
    Quack quack quack

Mr. Holly joined the group of campers who had gathered around Lucy and Susan. They were wet and shivering, but in good spirits.

Mr. Holly said, "Ladies, you don't know how happy I am that things turned out the way they did. Lucy, you are truly lucky that Susan was there to bring you to safety."

The campers at the park remembered Mr. Holly when he worked as the weather man for TV station WXYZ. He was known to be a miracle worker. Once he was able to push some dark clouds away from hitting Pleasant Village. When farmers needed rain, they called Mr. Holly to bring rain clouds.

Mr. Holly looked at what he could do to put everything back in order. First, he looked at Lucy and Susan standing there with wet clothes. He asked them to stand up straight. When he raised his hands he directed a warm wind to follow along after him. It took Mr. Holly only three trips to walk around Lucy and Susan, making them completely dry.

Mr. Holly then looked around and saw the lake and the river were larger than ever before. He then saw a mass of birds in the distance. When the birds got closer, Mr. Holly saw the birds were just crows. Mr. Holly said, "I have never had much use for crows, but I surely can use them now."

Next Mr. Holly raised his hands high and began calling "Caw, caw, caw." He directed the birds over the lake. The crows began flapping their wings so hard that the lake began to shrink and soon reduced its size back to a pond.

Then Mr. Holly raised his hands high over the river; and the crows flapped their wings there too. Soon the river started to shrink and reduced its size to just a stream.

The day after the "Big Rescue", Mr. Holly asked Susan and Lucy to come by the Pleasant Club House.

Susan showed up first. Mr. Holly carefully looked Susan over. There were no tears dripping down her face.

"Susan," said Mr. Holly, "you look great. No more sadness?"

"No more sadness", Susan replied.

"I'm really happy for you" said Mr. Holly. "I'm wondering where Lucy is now?"

"Ding, ding, ding-a-ling," shouted Lucy. "I heard you two talking and you mentioned my name."

Mr. Holly said, "I'm glad that you could meet me here. There are many people in town who want to know about the big rescue. They want to have a celebration party right here at Pleasant Park."

"Let's make sure the food committee knows we will prepare some blackberry cobblers," said Susan.

"And we need to let everyone know about the fruit and vegetable stand," said Lucy.

The celebration started with a picnic. There was a great display of fried chicken, hotdogs, potato salad, corn on the cob, and of course blackberry cobbler.

Then there was a time for games. There were baseball and hockey games for the grownups and for the children there was a sack race, a relay race, and a tug-of-war.

The highlight of the party came when people looked up in the sky and saw white, lacy clouds appearing. The clouds were gently dropping "stardust" in the air. As the stardust fell it formed a message which spelled out WE LOVE LUCY and WE LOVE SUSAN.

Then in Pleasant Village no one ever remembered anyone calling Lucy "Kooky Lucy" or calling Susan "Sobbing Susan" again.

www.ingramcontent.com/pod-product-compliance
Lightning Source LLC
Chambersburg PA
CBHW081355080526
44588CB00016B/2508